MORE THAN HYMNS 2

HYMN-ANTHEMS FOR
MIXED VOICE CHOIRS

SELECTED AND EDITED BY BARRY ROSE

NOVELLO

LONDON

FRONT COVER photograph of Wells Cathedral Girl Choristers and
Lay Vicars by Tony Bolton
BACK COVER photograph of Barry Rose by Timothy Hands

COVER DESIGN Miranda Harvey

MUSIC SETTING Barnes Music Engraving

NOV 040044
ISBN 0-7119-9394-7

© Copyright 2002 Novello & Company Ltd.
Published in Great Britain by Novello Publishing Limited.

HEAD OFFICE
14/15 Berners Street,
London W1T 3LJ
Tel. +44 (0) 20 7612 7400
Fax +44 (0) 20 7612 7546

SALES AND HIRE
Music Sales Limited,
Newmarket Road,
Bury St Edmunds,
Suffolk IP33 3YB
England
Tel +44 (0)1284 702600
Fax +44 (0)1284 768301

www.musicsales.com
e-mail: music@musicsales.co.uk

Be still, for the presence of the Lord; Christ be with you; Come down,
O Love divine; Crossing the bar; King of Glory; Let all mortal flesh;
Lord of all hopefulness; Morning glory, starlit sky; Now is the bitter
time and Thou art the way feature on the Lammas Records CD *More
than Hymns* (LAMM 149D) performed by the Choir of Wells Cathedral,
directed by Malcolm Archer, with Rupert Gough, organ

Contents

Preface

Hymns have long been the most enduring musical element in Christian worship, and choirs have good reason to be grateful for a wealth of metrical texts, ranging from the early Latin hymns to those in the more modern idiomatic English of the present day.

In most services, hymns are sung congregationally, but throughout the centuries, composers have been drawn to set new music to texts they have played or sung so often, or to arrange and extend well-loved tunes for use as choir anthems.

This, then, is the basis on which we now welcome you to *More Than Hymns* – a two-volume collection which will bring new and existing anthem-style arrangements to your choir library, together with the original music of composers who have drawn their inspiration from the poetry of hymnody.

With texts of prayer and praise, hope and consolation, coupled with memorable melodies, we hope that there is something here for all choirs who lead worship.

I am grateful to my fellow choral advisers at Novello for their help and advice and to Elizabeth Robinson for her painstaking preparation of these two volumes.

Barry Rose
Somerset, February 2002

Notes on the music

Be still, for the presence of the Lord · David Evans (b. 1957), arr. Indra Hughes (b. 1968)

Although written less than twenty years ago, *Be still, for the presence of the Lord* is already one of the most popular of all hymns. The text is based on Genesis 28, verses 16-17 – the story of Jacob at Bethel – 'surely the Lord is in this place, and I knew it not ... how awesome is this place'. The words and music were written by David Evans in his home city of Winchester, and his memorable tune has been arranged for this book by Blackburn-born Indra Hughes, now resident in Auckland, New Zealand, where he is a well-known conductor, organist and broadcaster.

Throughout this collection you will find key words which point to the approach the singers should take, and the clues here are in the arranger's markings of *tranquillo* and *espressivo*. Follow these and you'll successfully paint the 'stillness' in the opening line and through your expressive singing bring all of the words to life, so that they mean something to your listeners. Verse 2 is intended for unaccompanied choirs, but it could be accompanied gently as a support to less experienced singers. In the last verse, please take care that the descant does not end up, as so often happens, louder than the all-important message of the text. The arranger has added an Amen, with some musical quotes from the melody in the soprano line.

Christ be with you · Barry Rose (b. 1934)

The text is the central section of the hymn *I bind unto myself today*, known as St. Patrick's Breastplate. Mrs. C.F. Alexander (1818-95) made her translation of the ancient poem in 1889, and her version uses the personal pronoun – 'Christ be with me'. At the 1995 enthronement of the Bishop of St. Albans, he asked for three choral versions of this text to be sung at different points in the service, using 'Christ be with me', 'Christ be with us', and 'Christ be with you'. I could only find two settings of the music, so agreed to write the third for the occasion. The optional introduction was included to set the mood, to link the end of the congregational hymn 'When I survey the wondrous Cross' to this new choral setting. The introduction is, therefore dispensable, making a complete unaccompanied short anthem.
It needs to be sung very *legato* and with a rise and fall within the phrases. Your choir will need to take care over the balance between the parts in bar 14 (so that the text remains clear) and you will also need to rehearse bar 16 carefully, for tuning in all parts.

Come down, O Love divine · William Harris (1883-1973)

The English translation of Bianco's fifteenth century text dates from 1851 and has since appeared in many hymn books, usually coupled with Ralph Vaughan Williams' tune *Down Ampney*. William Harris named his tune after the Somerset village of North Petherton and it was used in the original 1950 edition of *Hymns Ancient and Modern*; in 1965 he extended it into the anthem-form included here.

The melody is immediately appealing and successfully brings the text to life with its alternation between triple and quadruple time. As with so many choral compositions, you will find that some of the note values need to be shortened at the ends of phrases, in order to give the singers time to breathe and start the next lead in time. It is possible to allow a little *allargando* in the organ part in bar 67 before reverting to the original key and melody, with its optional descant on page 15. Choir directors always need to help their singers achieve the right mood in performance, and if I had to use just one word to explain how to sing the piece, it would be 'fervently'!

Crossing the Bar · Charles Hubert Hastings Parry (1848-1918)

This is the work of two consummate craftsmen, poet and composer. Alfred, Lord Tennyson (1809-92) wrote his poem in 1889 at his home by the sea at Farringford, Isle of Wight. With its nautical terminology, its meaning has often been misinterpreted, the 'Pilot' being described by the author as 'that Divine and Unseen who is always guiding us' ... (The 'bar' is an offshore ridge of sand, mud, or shingle across the mouth of a river, bay or harbour.) Parry's music perfectly matches the irregular metre of the poem and has an unforgettable melody. It is an exquisite miniature which demands great flexibility within the rhythm and phrasing. I was once told that it is often harder to interpret so-called simple four-part pieces than much larger anthems – and how right that is! You may need to persuade your choir of this, although astute singers will immediately recognise the genius of both author and composer.

Forty days and forty nights · Martin Herbst, arr. Harrison Oxley (b. 1933)

The text of this well-loved Lenten hymn was written in 1856 whilst the author, the Rev. George Smyttan (1822-70) was Rector of Hawksworth, Nottingham, and it was later altered by the editors before being included in several well-known hymnals. Harrison Oxley's effective and extended anthem version uses the associated seventeenth century German tune, sometimes attributed to Martin Herbst (1654-81) and brings a new freedom from the usually stolid congregational singing. The choral parts in verse 3 may feel quite astringent when rehearsed on their own. But they paint the text so well and when put with the accompaniment, they add to the meaning of what is being sung, as does the strong C minor fourth verse, suitably set for the tenors and basses. This is one of those occasions when you and your singers should think of two, rather than four beats in each bar, otherwise you may end up with the weakest syllables of the words becoming the strongest ones.

Hail, gladdening Light · Hugh Blair (1864-1932)

Here is one of the oldest Christian hymns, translated by John Keble (1792-1866). The words are the *Phos Hilaron* (candlelight hymn) and date from third century Greece, where they were probably sung at the lighting of the lamps for the evening service. Hugh Blair's setting was written in 1927 whilst he was organist of Holy Trinity Church, Marylebone, London, and it uses only verse 1 and part of verse 3, with an Amen. His music is tuneful, sonorous and somewhat similar in harmonic content to his well-known Evening Service in B minor. It is a suitable introit or anthem for Evensong and will appeal to SATB choirs who want to sing these words in a simple, yet effective anthem setting.

Here, O my Lord, I see thee face to face · Barry Rose (b. 1934)

This was originally an upper voice anthem for an American church choir of boys and girls, and the SATB harmonisation has been made for inclusion in this book. The text of this Communion hymn was written in 1855 by the Scottish Free Church minister, Dr. Horatius Bonar. It originally had ten verses, but this setting uses the three verses which appear in most hymnals. I wrote a melody which the boys and girls could learn quickly, just before they were due to leave for a visit to the United Kingdom. Perhaps the real challenge is for your choir not just to understand the poem, but also to get that meaning across to the listening congregation. How often have I heard the opening phrase sounding as 'Hero my Lord'. There needs to be some careful articulation here, as there does in such places as bars 6-7 ('and handle'), bar 10 ('and all'). I'm sure you'll soon see (and hear) the problems which can be created by lack of careful attention to framing of the words!

King of glory, King of peace · Henry Walford Davies (1869-1941)

One of the most influential choirmasters of the twentieth century, Henry Walford Davies wrote this tuneful anthem whilst he was at the Temple Church, London between 1898 and 1919. It comes from a set of fourteen *Spiritual Songs*. It is an irrepressibly happy setting of words by the seventeenth century priest and poet, George Herbert, and perfectly catches the mood of the poem; note the composer's direction, *Allegro felice* (sprightly and happy). A simplified version of the music has been previously published, but here we reproduce it as Walford Davies wrote it. You will find that, even with a small and inexperienced choir, it will be quite easy to learn, given some careful and detailed rehearsal. Although it is not marked, it would be possible to double the voice parts in the unaccompanied sections, if this would add some security for the singers. The introduction and interludes play an important part in setting the right mood for the following verse, and pianists/organists should take care to observe carefully the phrasing and other markings.

Let all mortal flesh keep silence · 17th century French carol, arr. Stephen Jackson (b. 1951)

The words are from the 4th century Liturgy of St. James, translated in 1868 and then put into verse by the Rev. Gerard Moultrie (1829-85), chaplain of Shrewsbury School. The now well-known melody was included in the *English Hymnal* of 1906, where it is described as a French carol from the seventeenth century. It is unusual in that it does not have the usual dance-like feel often associated with carol melodies, especially in this minor key, but nevertheless it seems to be a perfect match for the words.

Stephen Jackson's exciting setting embraces some unexpected key changes and also requires three soprano parts (one being a semi-chorus) for a few bars (64-72). The mystical mood is set by the organ accompaniment, and in teaching this piece to your choir, it would be a good idea to get them used to the two bars preceding each verse, so that they can learn to adapt to the new tonality at the key changes. As a former member of the BBC Singers and now Director of the BBC Symphony Chorus, Jackson writes accessible and logical lines for every part in the choir, which can be learnt in one or two rehearsals. It is the accompanist who will need to do some thorough work in preparing some of the adventurous and highly effective chord sequences.

(See also *More than Hymns Volume 1* for an unaccompanied choir arrangement of this melody and words by Rogers Covey-Crump)

Lord of all hopefulness · Irish trad., arr. Barry Rose (b. 1934)

Aptly described as 'an all-day hymn', the words were specially written in 1932 for inclusion in the new *Songs of Praise* hymnbook. The author was Jan Struther, the pen name and maiden name of Mrs. Joyce Placzek, who became well known through her wartime novel, *Mrs. Miniver*.

The music, which has long been associated with this hymn, is the melody of a traditional Irish folk song, *With my love on the road*. For this book, I have extended an arrangement of verses 2 and 4 originally made in 1979 for a wedding service. Perhaps the key word here is *flowing*, and it will help your singers if they think of one beat in each bar, rather than three. In verse 2, it is possible for a solo baritone to sing the 1st bass and for the other parts to vocalise gently – either by humming or on *'oo'*. The gentleness of the last verse can easily be disturbed by an over-zealous group on the descant: this really is meant for a *few* voices, to help create the feeling of calm and peace.

Lord of the Dance · Sydney Carter (b. 1915), arr. John Barnard (b. 1948)

The descriptive and popular text, spanning our Lord's birth, crucifixion, resurrection and ascension, owes much of its popularity to the inspired coupling with a melody which originated from the Shaker sect, in mid-nineteenth century North America. It was used by Aaron Copland in his 1944 ballet *Appalachian Spring*, and five years later, he arranged it for solo voice and piano.

Sydney Carter wrote *Lord of the Dance* in 1963 and it has been a favourite congregational hymn ever since. Now John Barnard gives us his arrangement for choir and organ, vividly bringing the dancing mood to life from the very first organ introduction. It is an effervescent setting, full of colour and drive, and yet demanding a real sense of word interpretation from your choir. *Rhythmic vitality* are key words for a successful performance and I'm sure everyone who sings or plays it will enjoy this new treatment of an old favourite.

Love's redeeming work is done · Bryan Kelly (b. 1934)

This new setting is a far cry from the four-square tune usually associated with these Eastertide words of Charles Wesley (1707-88). Originally written as an eleven verse hymn, most hymn book editors have since omitted the first verse (which begins 'Christ the Lord is risen today'), probably thinking it would cause confusion with the better known 'Jesus Christ is risen today'.

Bryan Kelly studied composition at the Royal College of Music and later returned there to teach. His 1965 setting of the Evening Canticles based on Latin-American rhythms (published by Novello) remains a favourite amongst many church and cathedral choirs, and there is a similar rhythmic energy to be found in *Love's redeeming work is done*. From the very outset, there is a festive feeling, and an infectiously rhythmic accompaniment to verse 2 (*'Vain the stone'*). The choir needs to be very precise here, and also at the similar passage at the beginning of verse 4. The joyful ending to a joyful text should be reflected on the faces of the performers. Now there's a challenge, for too many choirs look the same in Passiontide and Easter music! Smile, and hear (and feel) the difference.

Morning glory, starlit sky · Barry Rose (b. 1934)

This music was written for a BBC Radio 4 Daily Service, broadcast live from a basement studio in Broadcasting House and sung by eight members of the BBC Singers; the request was for an unaccompanied setting. The text is part of a longer poem by Canon W.H. Vanstone (1923-99), *Love's endeavour, Love's expense*, and it is now published in many hymn books in the shortened form given here. Although there is room for expression and word-painting in the singing, the key word should be *simply*, for what is basically a simple folk-like melody; clarity in the sound is all important. There is one catch-point which may need rehearsal:– the first note of bar 35 goes down to A flat, whereas in the soprano part and tenor solo in previous verses it went up to C. The opening and closing verses work equally well with a soloist or semi-chorus.

My Dancing Day · trad., arr. Gerald Near (b. 1942)

Historically, carols are linked with dancing, and nowhere is this link more apparent than in this lively dance-like melody, set to part of a carol from Cornwall, UK, and first published in 1833. The 'dancing day' probably refers to a three day religious festival in which the participants acted out the poem with its complete life-cycle of

Christ, though the words used in this setting only cover the festival of Christmas.

Gerald Near is a prolific American composer and church musician and in this arrangement, he immediately catches the mood of both words and music with a jaunty introduction, leading to the well-known tune. The key word for the singers has to be *lightness* – the words and music dance along. Music in 6/8 time is often difficult to keep in strict rhythm without sounding grabbed at the ends of phrases, and it may help if your choir can think of phrases of two bar length (12/8) rather than the shorter printed bars. I have always maintained that verse 2 ('Then was I born') is a real test of a choir's ability to frame and sing the words well, and it might be worth asking your singers to say this in time before they sing it, and perhaps ask one of them to stand at the back of the church as their critic – this can be very revealing!

Now is the bitter time · J.W. Franck (1644-c.1710), arr. Gavin Williams (b. 1942)

Here is one of those pieces in which words and music are exactly matched, giving us a poignant reminder of the meaning of Passiontide and Christ's suffering on the Cross.

The text, originally two verses in German, was written by the Hamburg clergyman Heinrich Elmenhorst (1632-1704) and set to music for solo voice and instrumental accompaniment by Johann Wolfgang Franck, whilst he was chapel choirmaster at Ansbach between 1673 and 1679.

This version was made by Gavin Williams in 1967 for the choir of Guildford Cathedral, and transposes the music up a minor third from its original key of A minor. It needs to be sung with great affection and understanding, and the more you sing it, the more you realise how beautifully the music paints the text, for instance, 'weep our sad tears now in ceaseless flow', and 'Jesu my Lord doth bow his head'. There needs to be great care in the tuning of the mean (alto and tenor) parts, especially in such places as tenors in bars 3-4 and altos in bar 16.

O sons and daughters let us sing · arr. Henry Walford Davies (1869-1941)

The words and music date from late fifteenth century France and are said to be by a monk, who, with his brethren, probably danced around on Easter Day, singing this cheerful tune in celebration of Christ's resurrection. This version is another from Henry Walford Davies's *Spiritual Songs* (see also *King of Glory*) and is an anthem-style arrangement to the 1851 English translation by John Mason Neale (1818-66).

The opening instruction 'joyously' reminds

us to keep this moving, with a dance-like feel. Perhaps ask your singers to think of two beats in a bar, to help point the rhythmic impulse. In some performances I've heard, there has been a very slight gap between the verses, and we have taken the liberty of inserting a comma in the music at these points. It is also quite usual to have a slight *allargando* in bar 38 before setting off on the last verse, perhaps at a slightly steadier tempo. The second sopranos need to be the strongest part in the last two bars, since they complete the melody which has previously been passed to the basses, and then to the whole choir.

Thou art the way · Christopher Steel (1938-91)

Here is a text with an interesting history, for it had the distinction of being the only hymn by an American author to be included in the first edition of *Hymns Ancient and Modern*, in 1861. It was written by Bishop George Washington Doane (1799-1859) whilst he was Rector of St. Mary's Church, Burlington, New Jersey, probably as a teaching aid to the boys and girls in two local schools he founded. He may have drawn his inspiration from the fourteenth chapter of St. John's Gospel, or from George Herbert's *The Call* – 'Come, my way, my truth, my life'.

In his setting, Christopher Steel gives us a strong, logical, and memorable tune, with some more 'modern' effects being created by adventurous chords in the accompaniment. The musical construction allows the text to grow in intensity until the major key of the last verse, which gathers together the Way, the Truth and the Life. In the absence of a confident soloist, it is possible to have all the tenors and basses singing the first verse, and care should be taken that the melody is not obscured by the upper parts at bars 29-36 and especially in the descant above verse 3.

Perhaps I could end both these volumes with a final plea for care over the way you sing the words in every hymn and anthem. Remember that they were there before the music.

Happy singing!

Barry Rose

Small-sized notes in the accompaniments are for rehearsal purposes only.

Be still, for the presence of the Lord

Words and melody by David J. Evans,
arr. Indra Hughes

3

4

Christ be with you

Attrib. St. Patrick,
tr. Mrs. C.F. Alexander

Barry Rose

Bars 1–4 are an optional introduction.

Come down, O Love divine

Hymn-anthem on the tune 'North Petherton'

Bianco da Siena,
tr. R.F. Littledale

William H. Harris

With-in my heart ap - pear, And kin - dle it, thy ho - ly flame be -

- stow - ing.

Ped.

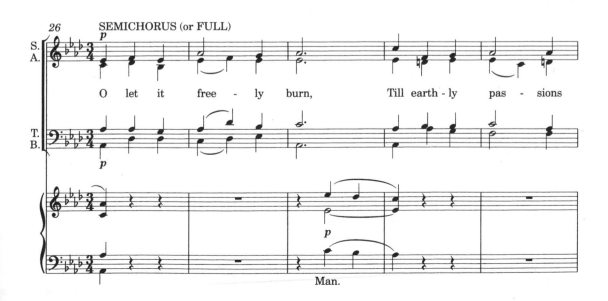

SEMICHORUS (or FULL)

S.
A.

O let it free - ly burn, Till earth - ly pas - sions

T.
B.

Man.

12

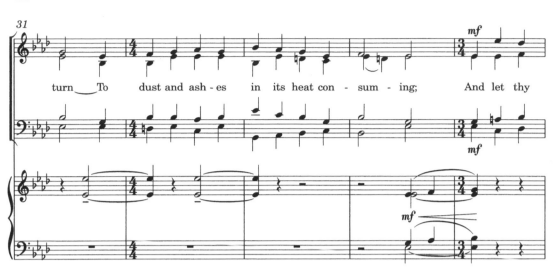

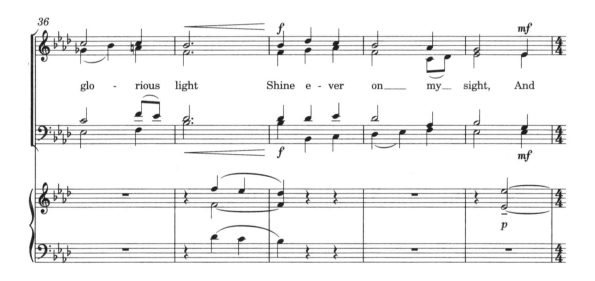

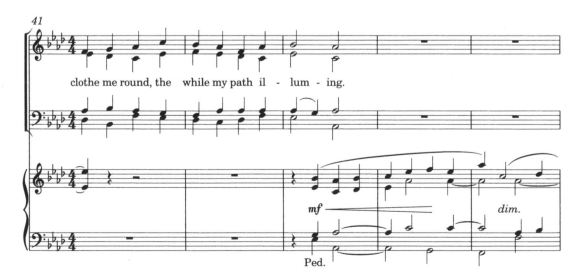

Let ho - ly cha - ri - ty   Mine out-ward

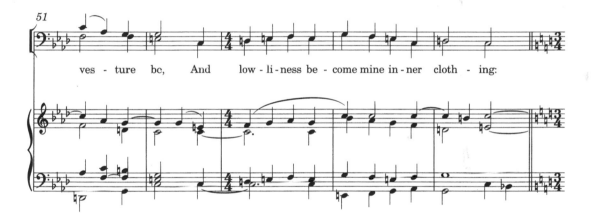

ves - ture be,   And   low - li - ness be - come mine in - ner cloth - ing:

True low - li - ness   of   heart,   Which takes the   hum - bler

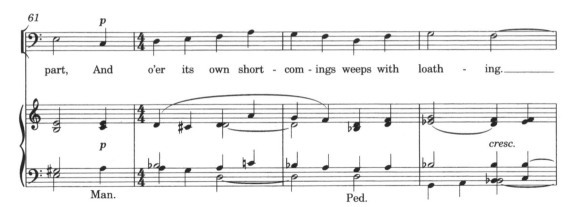

part, And o'er its own short - com - ings weeps with loath - ing.

Man.   Ped.

And so the yearn - ing

(unis.)

strong, With which the soul__ will long, Shall far out - pass the

pow'r of hu-man tell - ing; For none can guess its grace,

Till he be - come_ the_ place Where - in the Ho - ly Spi - rit makes his

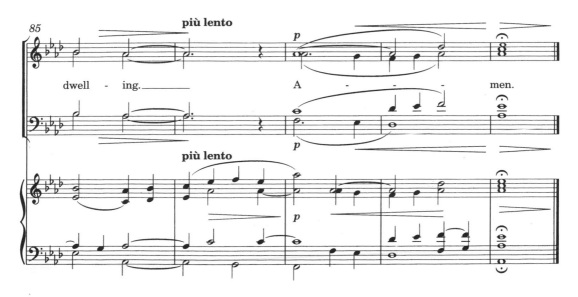

dwell - ing._____ A - - - men.

Crossing the bar

Alfred Lord Tennyson

C.H.H. Parry

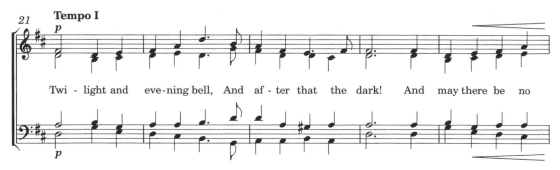

Twi - light and eve-ning bell, And af - ter that the dark! And may there be no

sad - ness of fare - well, When I_____ em - bark; For tho' from out our

bourne of Time and Place The flood may bear me far, I hope to see my

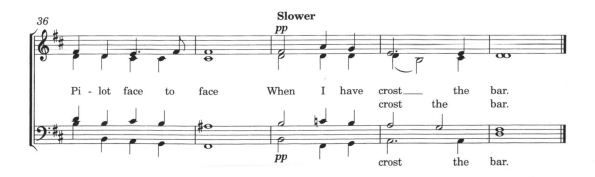

Pi - lot face to face When I have crost_____ the bar.
crost the bar.
crost the bar.

18

Forty days and forty nights

G.H. Smyttan and Francis Pott

Melody attrib. Martin Herbst,
arr. Harrison Oxley

20

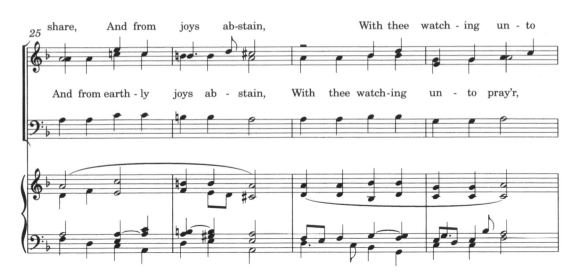

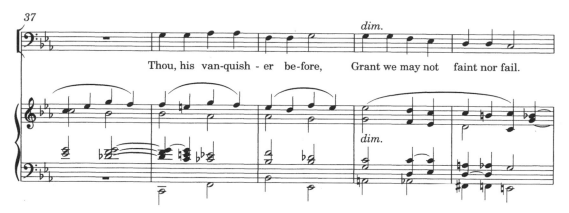

Thou, his van-quish - er be-fore, Grant we may not faint nor fail.

5. So shall we have peace di - vine, Ho - lier glad-ness ours shall be,

Round us too shall an-gels shine, Such as mi - ni - ster'd to thee.

22

Hail, gladdening Light

John Keble

Hugh Blair

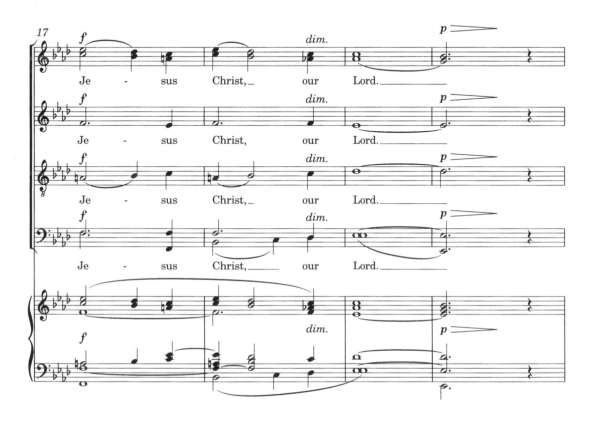

26

For Vincent Edwards and the Choristers of Saint Paul's Church, Fairfield, USA

Here, O my Lord

Horatius Bonar

Barry Rose

28

*mm or oo
†a few sopranos, the remainder sing with altos.

King of Glory

George Herbert

Henry Walford Davies

* or Full

* or Full

32

* or Full

Let all mortal flesh keep silence

Liturgy of St. James
tr. Gerard Moultrie

Picardy – 17th century French carol
'Jésus Christ s'habille en pauvre'
arr. Stephen Jackson

Lord of lords, in hu - man_ ves - ture, In the bo - dy and the_

Lord of lords, in hu - man_ ves - ture, In the bo - dy and the_

Gt. solo

blood: He will give to all the faith - ful His own self for

blood: He will give to all the faith - ful His own self for

heav'n - ly_ food.

heav'n - ly_ food.

Ch.

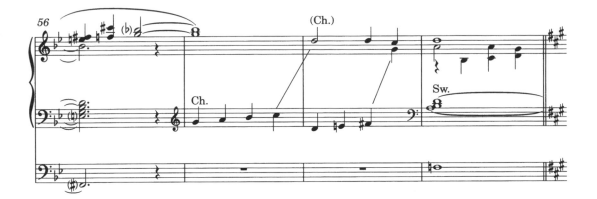

68

8' & 16'

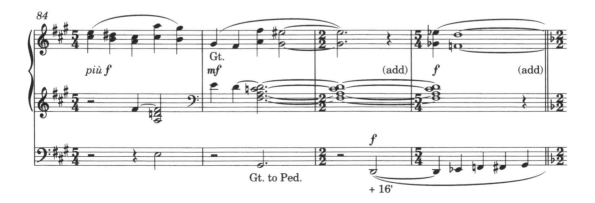

Cease - less - ly they cry, Al - - le -

As with cease-less voice they_ cry, Al - le - lu - ia, Al - le -

As with cease-less voice they_ cry, Al - le - lu - ia, Al - le -

+reeds

-lu - - - ia, Al - le - lu - ia, Lord most high!

-lu - - ia, Al - le - lu - ia, Lord most_ high!

-lu - - ia, Al - le - lu - ia, Lord most_ high!

rit.

Lord of all hopefulness

Jan Struther

Irish trad.,
arr. Barry Rose

give us, we pray, Your strength in our hearts, Lord, at the noon of the day.

give us, we pray, Your strength in our hearts, Lord, at the noon of the day.

give us, we pray, Your strength in our hearts, Lord, at the noon of the day.

give us, we pray, Your strength in our hearts, Lord, at the noon of the day.

3. Lord of all kind-li-ness, Lord of all grace, Your hands swift to

wel-come, your arms to em-brace, Be there at our hom-ing and

50

Lord of the dance

Sydney Carter

Shaker tune, adapted Sydney Carter,
arr. John Barnard

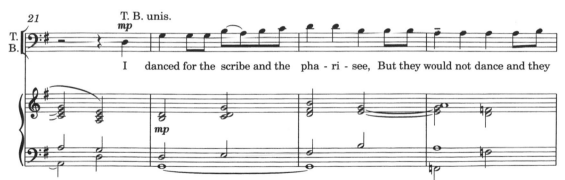

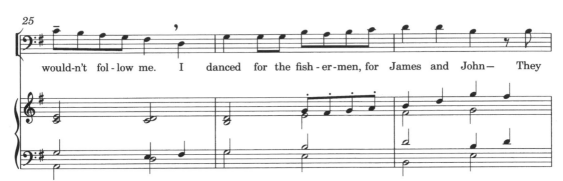

wouldn't fol-low me. I danced for the fish-er-men, for James and John— They

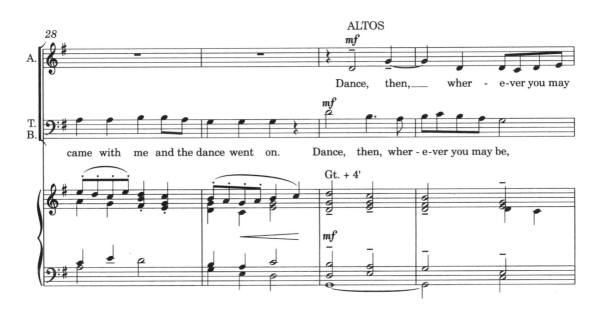

ALTOS

Dance, then,___ wher - e-ver you may

came with me and the dance went on. Dance, then, wher - e-ver you may be,

Gt. + 4'

be, I am the Lord of the Dance, said he, And I'll lead you

I am the Lord of the Dance, said he, And I'll lead you all, wher -

all, wher - e - ver you may be, I'll lead you in the Dance, said he.

- e - ver you may be, And I'll lead you all in the Dance, said he.

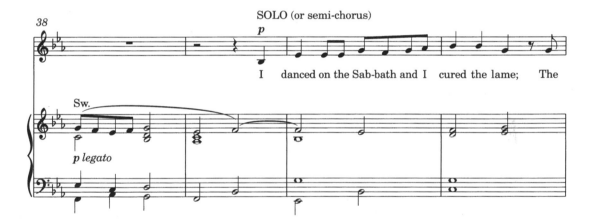

SOLO (or semi-chorus)

I danced on the Sab-bath and I cured the lame; The

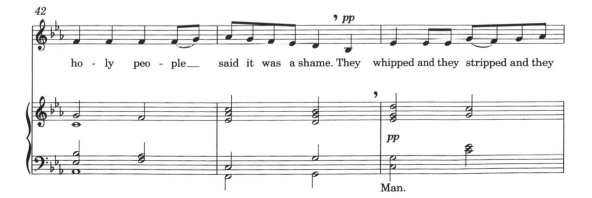

ho - ly peo - ple__ said it was a shame. They whipped and they stripped and they

I danced on a Fri-day when the sky turned black — It's

hard to dance with the de-vil on your back. They bu-ried my bo-dy and they

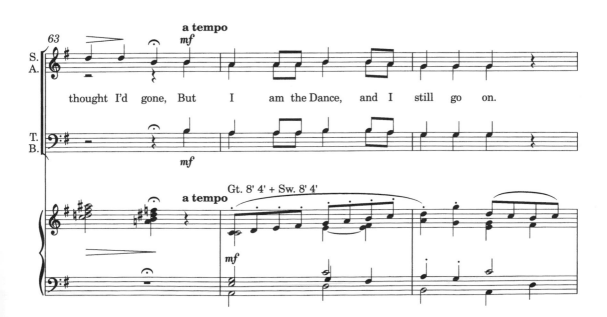

thought I'd gone, But I am the Dance, and I still go on.

Dance, then, wher-e-ver you may be, I am the Lord of the

S. Dance, said he, And I'll lead you all, wher-e-ver you may be, And I'll lead you all in the

A. Dance, said he, And I'll lead you all, wher-e-ver you may be,___ in the

T.
B. Dance, said he, And I'll lead you all, wher-e-ver you may_ be,___ in the_

Dance, said he.

Dance, said he.

Dance, said he.

Gt. add 8' + 2'

mf

cresc.

Man.

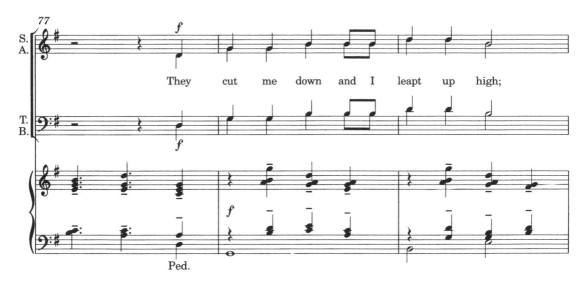

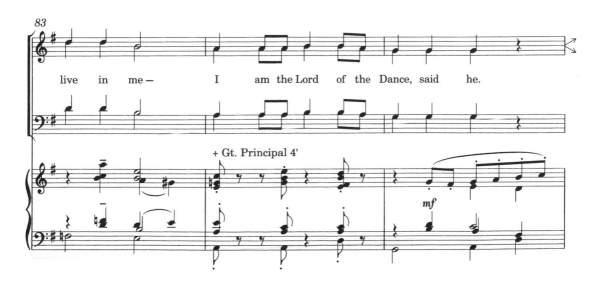

Love's redeeming work is done

Charles Wesley

Bryan Kelly

For Stephen Oliver and the BBC Singers

Morning glory, starlit sky
(*Love's endeavour, Love's expense*)

W. H. Vanstone

Barry Rose

- more, ____ gives with zeal, ____ with ea - ger hands, ____ spares not,

keeps not, all out - pours, ___ ven-tures all, its all ex - pends. ___

SOLO
Drained is

S.
A.

mm _____ mm ___

(T. SOLO)

love in mak-ing full, bound in set - ting o-thers free, poor in

mm ___

T.
B.

mm _____ mm ___

_____ There-fore

mak - ing ma-ny rich, weak in giv - ing power to be. ___ There-fore

mm _____

_____ There-fore

he who shows us God___ help-less hangs___ u-pon the tree;___ and the

nails and crown of thorns___ tell what___ love must

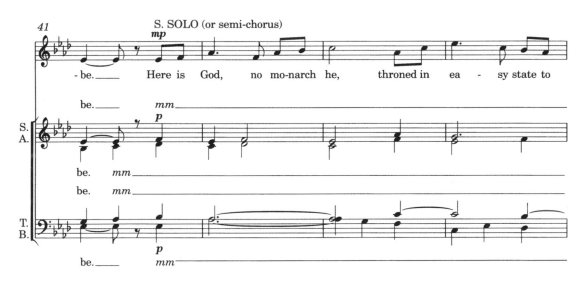

-be.___ Here is God, no mo-narch he, throned in ea-sy state to

be.___ mm

be. mm

be. mm

be.___ mm

reign; here is God, whose arms of love, ach-ing, spent, the world sus-tain.

___ mm

My dancing day

Melody and text from William Sandys,
Christmas Carols Ancient and Modern, 1833

English trad.,
arr. Gerald Near

68

* cue size notes for rehearsal only

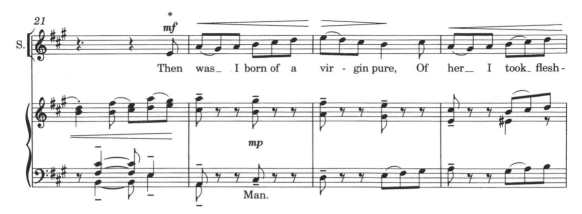

Then was_ I born of a vir-gin pure, Of her_ I took_ flesh-

Man.

-ly_ sub-stance; Thus was I knit to man's na-ture, To call my true_ love

to_ my dance: Sing O my love, O_ my love, my love, my love; This

Sing O my love,_ O_ my love, my love, my love; This

to_ my dance: Sing O my love,_ O_ my love; my love; This

Sing O my love, O my love, my love; This

* or Tenors

O__ my love, my love, my love;

O__ my love, my love, my love;

O__ my love, my love;

O my love, my love;

mf

Man.

This have I done for my__ true love.

This have I done for my true love.

This have I done for my true love.

This have I done for my true love.

f

mp

Ped.

Now is the bitter time

Original German by
Heinrich Elmenhorst

Johann Wolfgang Franck,
arr. Gavin Williams

74

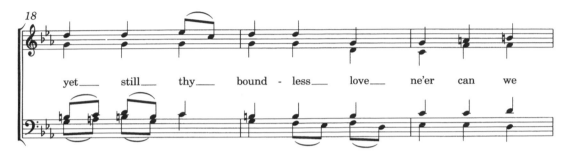

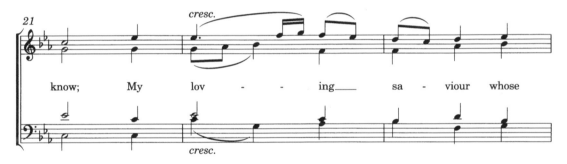

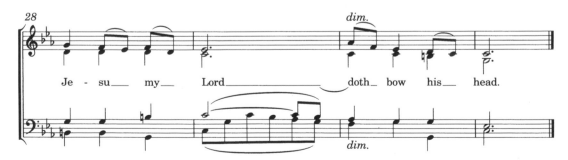

O sons and daughters let us sing!

Jean Tisserand,
tr. J. M. Neale and others

Proper for Easter Day,
harm. and arr. Henry Walford Davies

Thou art the way

Bishop G. W. Doane

Christopher Steel, Op. 39

80

* Organ ad lib.

82

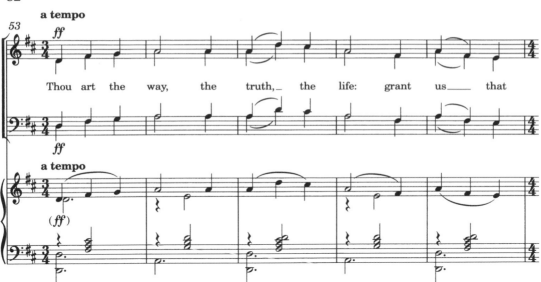

Thou art the way, the truth,_ the life: grant us_ that

way to know, That truth to keep, that life_ to

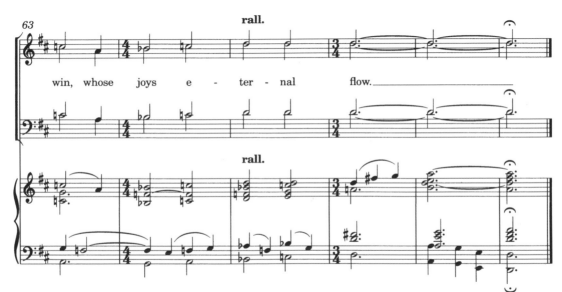

win, whose joys e - ter - nal flow._